Picture Dictionary

by John F. Onofrey

 CONTINENTAL PRESS

Acknowledgements

Design, Composition, and Art Direction: Crystal L. Crater

Corbis, Inc.: Cover, *bowl of soup, paintbrush, pineapple*; Title Page, *all*; Page 5, *rubber duck*; Page 6, *oval plate*; Page 10, *fall scene on calendar*; Page 11, *summer, fall*; Page 12, *lightning, rainbow*; Page 13, *cloudy, foggy, snowy*; Page 14, *pine*; Page 15, *sunflower seeds, cactus, tomato*; Page 16, *apple, blueberry*; Page 17, *orange, pineapple, strawberry*; Page 18, *beans, broccoli, carrots, corn*; Page 19, *lettuce, onion, potato*; Page 20, *bread, cereal, cheese, cookies, eggs, fish*; Page 21, *meat, pizza, soup, juice, milk*; Page 22, *boy, family*; Page 25, *sneakers*; Page 26, *lizard*; Page 29, *frog*; Page 31, *whale*; Page 34 *family room*; Page 37, *pen*; Page 38, *axe, flashlight*; Page 39, *paintbrush, scissors*; Page 40, *backhoe*; Page 41, *hair dryer, microwave oven, radio, sewing machine, toaster, vacuum, washer and dryer*; Page 42, *airplane*; Page 43, *truck*; Page 44, *astronaut*; Page 46, *firefighter*; Page 47, *office worker*; Page 48, *apartment house*; Page 49, *hotel*; Page 50, *museum, park, playground*; Page 51, *skyscrapers*; Page 52, *front of girls running, back of girls running, cold*; Page 53, *old sneakers, new sneakers, girl holding flower, otter*; Page 54, *empty and full recycle bins, newspaper, close-up of giraffe, far view of giraffes*; Page 55, *boy on bike, boy beside bike, bridges, hot air balloons*; Page 58, *eat, fall, fly, hit*; Page 60, *mix*; Page 61, *read*; Page 62, *skate, sleep, smell, swim*; Page 63, *talk, throw, walk, win*

PhotoDisc, Inc.: Cover, *boat, wagon, mittens, lion, kite, saw, chicken, guitar*; Page 4, *all*; Page 5, *eraser, sea shell, wagon, train, easel*; Page 6, *plate, chalkboard, checkerboard, sailboat, kite*; Page 9, *nickel, dime, quarter*; Page 11, *winter*; Page 12, *sun, crescent moon*; Page 13, *rainy, sunny*; Page 14, *maple seeds, maple, magnolia, walnut*; Page 15, *sunflower, corn, daisy*; Page 16, *banana, cherry, grape, lemon*; Page 17, *peach, pear, watermelon*; Page 18, *cabbage, celery*; Page 19, *pea, peppers, squash*; Page 20, *cake, hot dog, ice cream*; Page 21, *rice, sandwich, spaghetti, water*; Page 22, *man, girl, baby, woman*; Page 23, *boy*; Page 24, *cap, hat, mittens*; Page 25, *shoes*; Page 26, *cat, kitten, dog, puppy, horse*; Page 27 *all*; Page 28, *all*; Page 29, *dolphin, eagle, elephant, fox, giraffe, jellyfish, kangaroo*; Page 30, *all*; Page 31, *skunk, squirrel, tiger, wolf, zebra*; Page 34, *kitchen*; Page 35, *all*; Page 36, *all*; Page 37, *brush, chalk, crayons, pencil*; Page 38, *broom, fork, knife, hammer, mop*; Page 39, *rake, saw, screwdriver, shovel, spoon, wrench*; Page 40, *bulldozer, crane, lawn mower, snowblower, tractor*; Page 41, *telephone, television*; Page 42, *bicycle, elevated train*; Page 43, *motorcycle, subway, train*; Page 44, *carpenter, clerk, construction worker*; Page 45, *all*; Page 46, *engineer, farmer, hairdresser*; Page 47, *nurse, pilot, police officer, teacher*; Page 48, *airport, bank, city, factory*; Page 49, *garden, hospital, library*; Page 50, *ranch, restaurant*; Page 51, *school, stadium, store, supermarket*; Page 52, *horse, kitten, clean laundry, dirty laundry, empty grocery bag, full grocery bag, trees*; Page 53, *snake, worm, open and closed briefcases, leopard, turtle*; Page 54, *children standing in line, people at fence*; Page 55, *bike*; Page 56, *bend, blow, catch, clap, count*; Page 57, *all*; Page 58, *drink, hide*; Page 59, *hop, jump, knock, lift*; Page 60, *listen, look, meet, play*; Page 61, *pull, push, ride, run*; Page 62, *write*

EyeWire, Inc.: Page 11, *spring*; Page 12, *stars*; Page 13, *windy*; Page 26, *fishbowl, bird, hamster*; Page 41, *computer*; Page 42, *bus*; Page 43, *helicopter, van*; Page 51, *theater*; Page 52, *forest fire*; Page 56, *climb*; Page 59, *kick, kiss*; Page 60, *paint*, Page 61 *shout*; Page 62, *sing*

Fine Line Photography: Cover, *ten dollar bill*; Page 7, *boy with the letter r, girl with the letter c*; Page 8, *all*; Page 9, *penny, half-dollar, liberty dollar, all bills*; Page 24, *blouse, boots, coat, dress, gloves, jacket, pants*; Page 25, *scarf, shirt, shorts, skirt, socks, sweater, t-shirt*; Page 37, *markers*; Page 38, *drill*; page 42, *boat*; Page 48, *farm and barns, gym*; Page 63, *wash*

Photography by Glenn: Page 7, *girl with the letter f, boy with the letter a, boy with the letter v*

Image 100 Ltd.: Page 12, *full moon, clouds*; Page 14, *palm*; Page 48 *desert*

Illustrations by Michael Reilly: Page 10, *calendars*

Illustrations by Laurie Conley: Pages 32–33, *inside and outside of a house*

ISBN 978-0-8454-0959-6

The Continental Press, Inc., Elizabethtown, PA 17022

Table of Contents

Colors

black

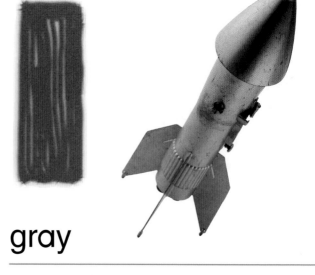

gray

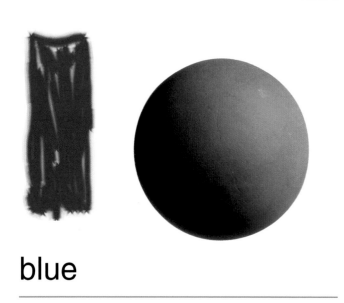

blue

green

brown

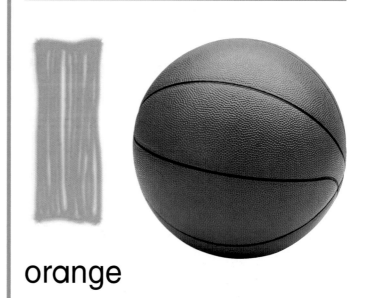

orange

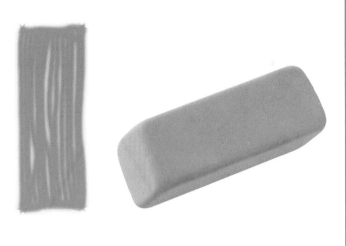

pink

tan

purple

white

red

yellow

Shapes

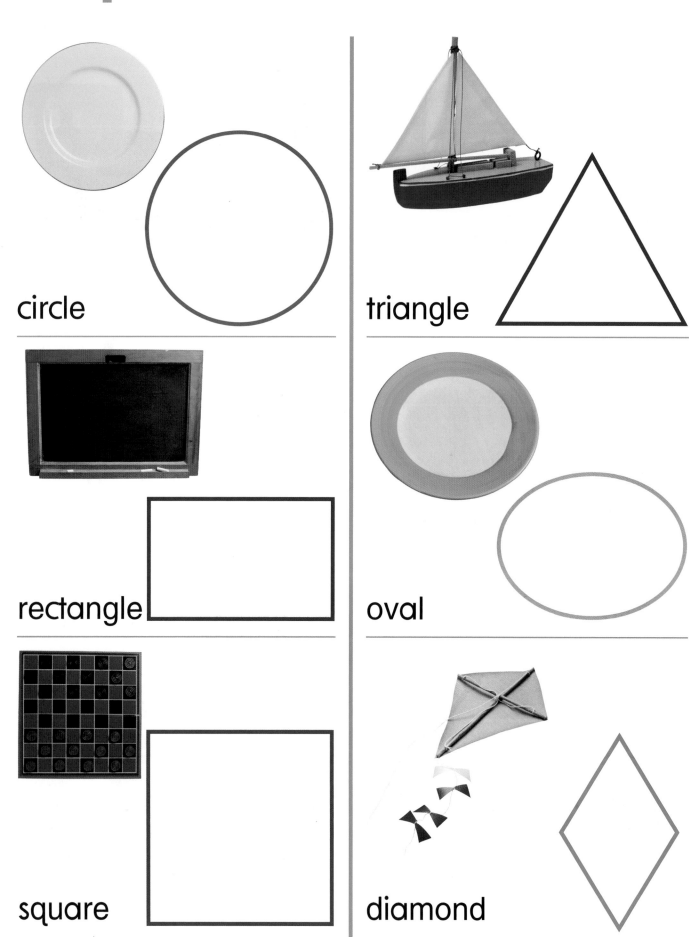

circle

triangle

rectangle

oval

square

diamond

Capital Letters

ABCDEFGHIJKLMNOPQRSTUVWXYZ

Lowercase Letters

abcdefghijklmnopqrstuvwxyz

Printing

This sentence is in printing.

Writing

This sentence is in handwriting.

Numbers

0 zero

1 one

2 two

3 three

4 four

5 five

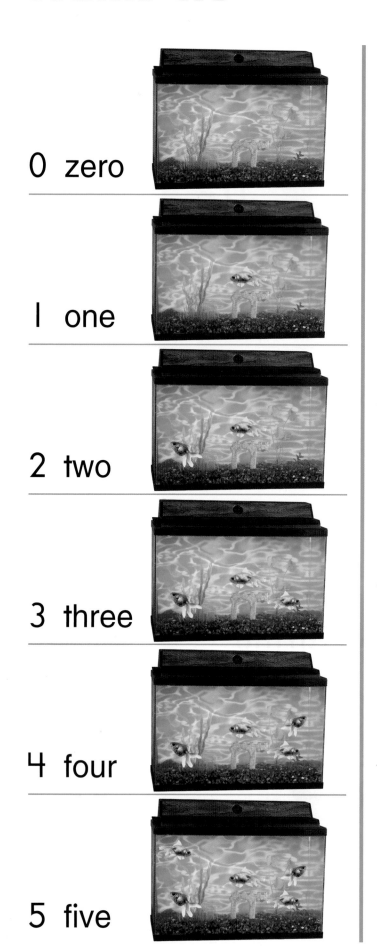

6 six

7 seven

8 eight

9 nine

10 ten

Money

Coins

penny 1¢

nickel 5¢

dime 10¢

quarter 25¢

half-dollar 50¢

dollar 100¢

Bills

one dollar $1.00

five dollars $5.00

ten dollars $10.00

twenty dollars $20.00

9

Months and Days

Months

January	July
February	August
March	September
April	October
May	November
June	December

Days

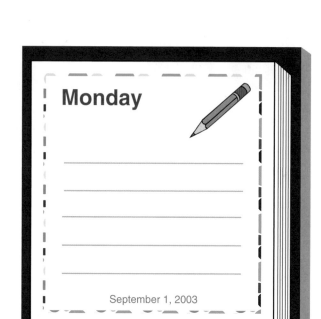

Sunday

Monday

Tuesday

Wednesday

Thursday

Friday

Saturday

Seasons of the Year

winter

summer

spring

fall

In the Sky

sun

clouds

crescent
moon

full
moon

lightning

stars

rainbow

12

cloudy

snowy

foggy

sunny

rainy

windy

Trees

seeds

limb

leaf

trunk

maple

palm

pine

magnolia

walnut

Plants

seeds

flower

leaf

stem

sunflower

cactus

corn

daisy

tomato

Fruits

apple

cherries

banana

grapes

blueberries

lemon

Fruits

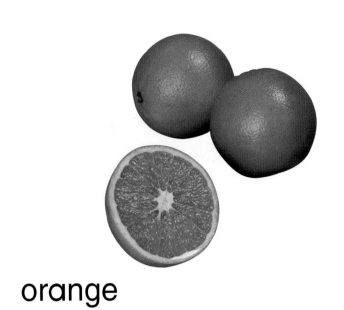

orange

pineapple

peaches

strawberries

pear

watermelon

Vegetables

beans

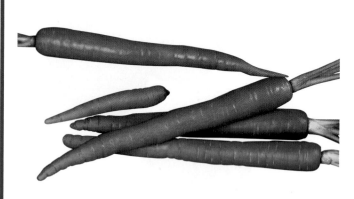

carrots

broccoli

celery

cabbage

corn

Vegetables

lettuce

peppers

onion

potato

pea

squash

More Food

bread

cake

cereal

cheese

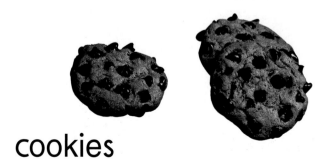
cookies

eggs

fish

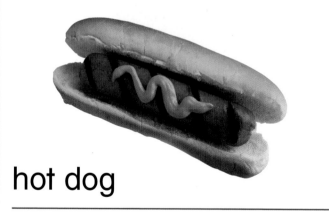
hot dog

ice cream

More Food

meat

pizza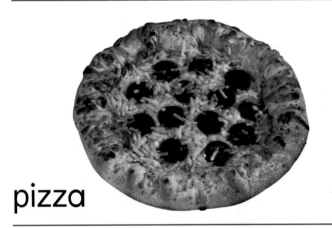

rice

sandwich

soup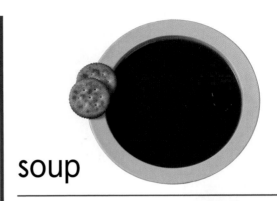

spaghetti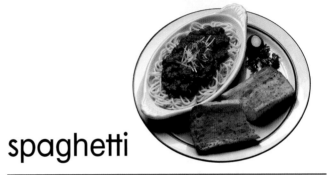

juice

milk

water

People and Families

girl

baby

man

boy

woman

father

mother

brother

sister

grandmother

grandfather

Your Body

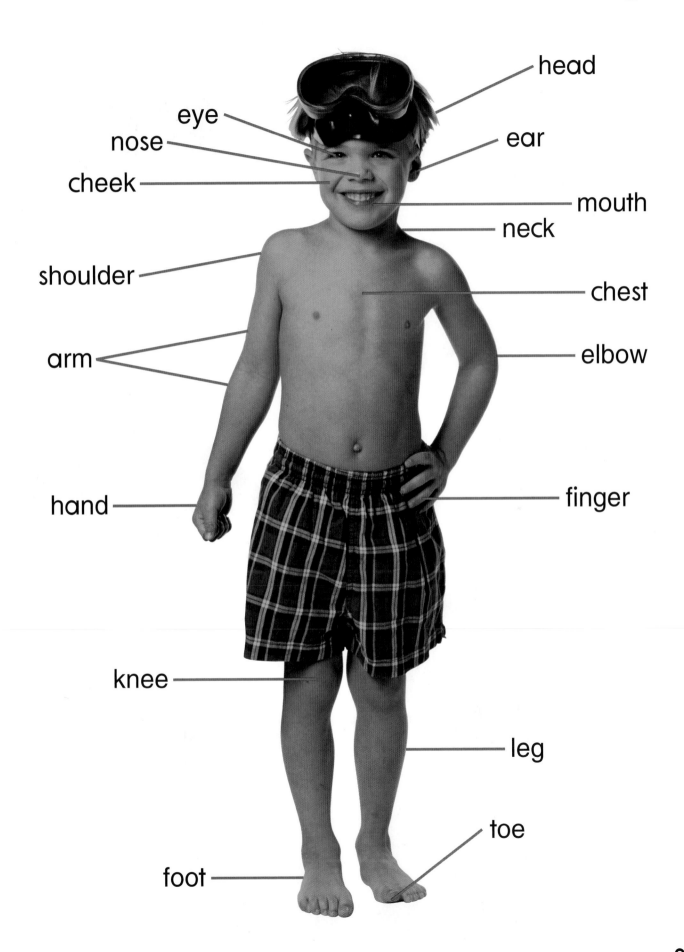

head

eye

nose

cheek

ear

mouth

neck

shoulder

chest

arm

elbow

hand

finger

knee

leg

toe

foot

Clothes

blouse

boots

cap

coat

dress

gloves

hat

jacket

mittens

pants

Clothes

scarf

shirt

shoes

shorts

skirt

sneakers

socks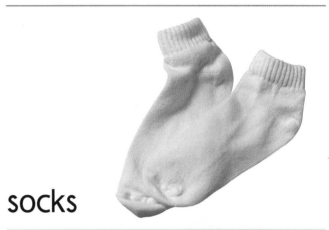

sweater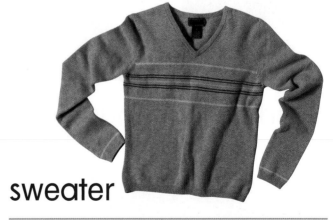

T-shirt

Pets

cat   kitten

dog   puppy

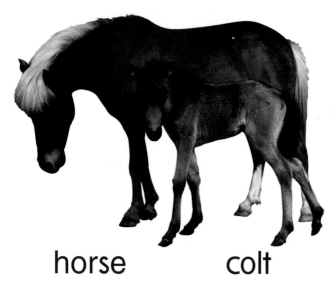

horse   colt

fish

bird

hamster

lizard

Farm Animals

chicken　　　chick

goat　　　kid

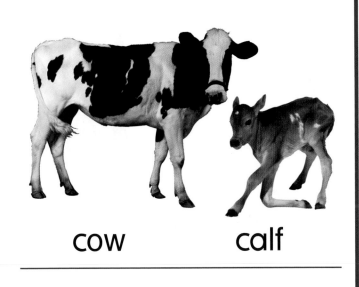

cow　　　calf

pig　　　piglet

duck　　　duckling

sheep　　　lamb

Wild Animals

alligator

butterfly

bat

camel

bear

crab

beaver

deer

dolphin

frog

eagle

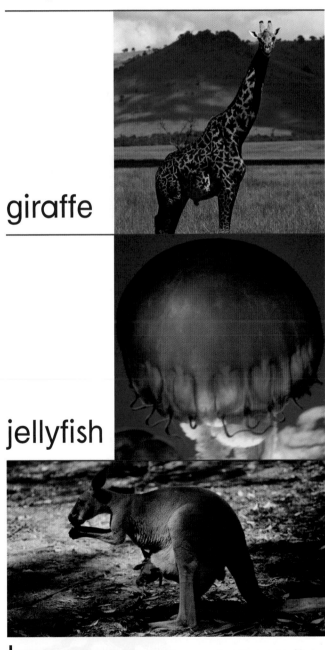

giraffe

elephant

jellyfish

fox

kangaroo

Wild Animals

lion

rabbit

monkey

raccoon

owl

penguins

snail

snake

Wild Animals

skunk

whale

squirrel

tiger

wolf

zebra

The Outside of a House

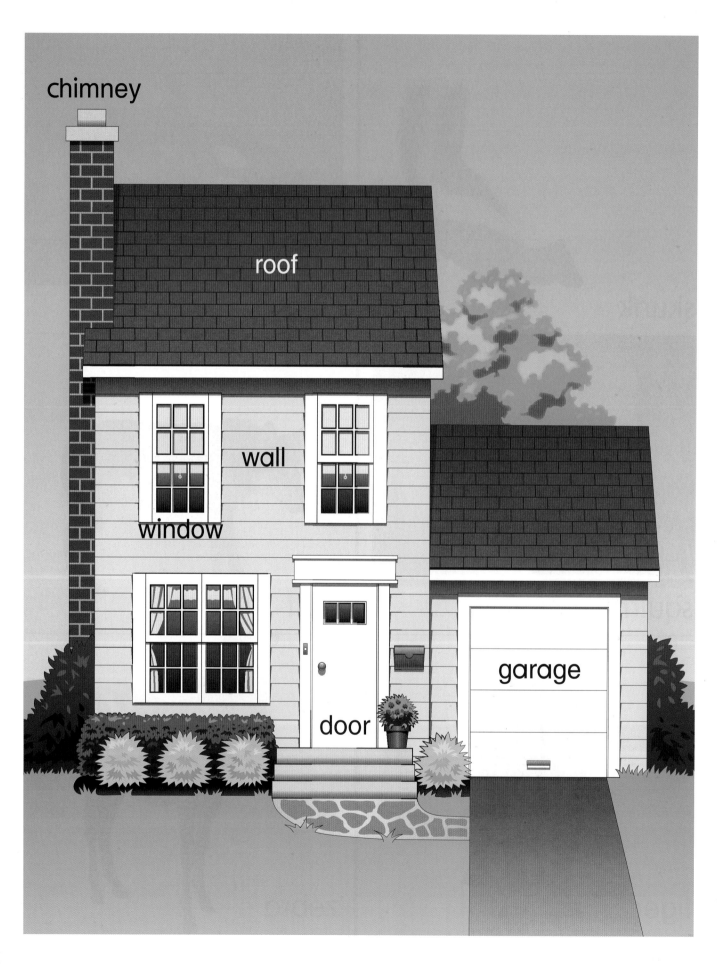

chimney

roof

wall

window

door

garage

The Inside of a House

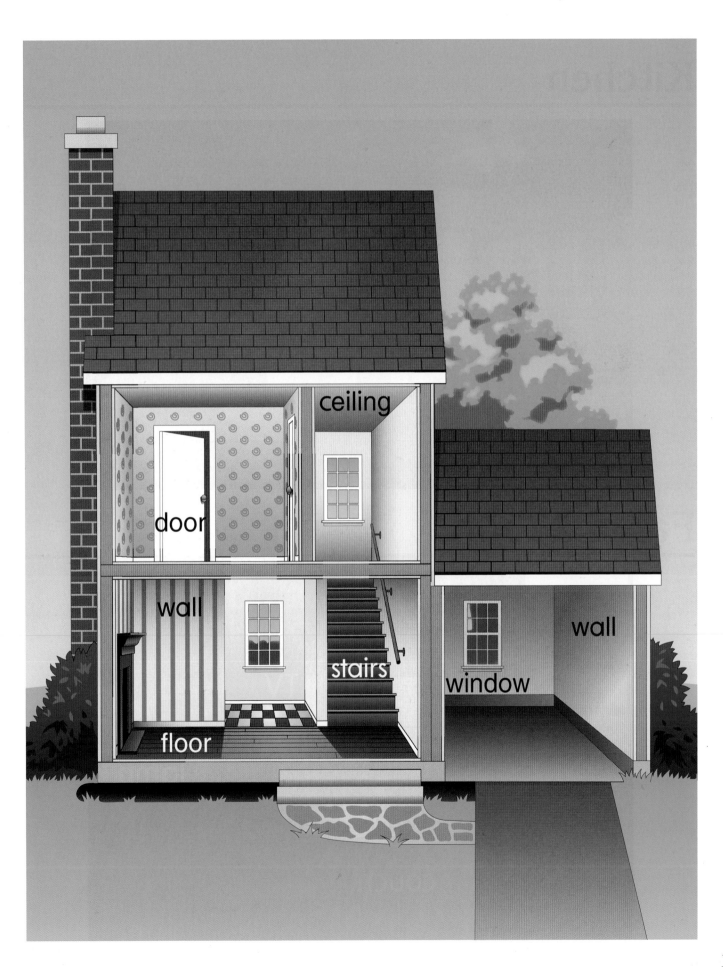

Rooms and Furniture

Kitchen

table

refrigerator

stove

sink

chairs

Family Room

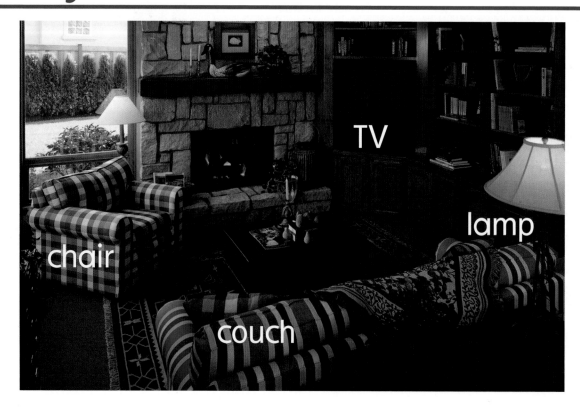

TV

lamp

chair

couch

Rooms and Furniture

Bedroom

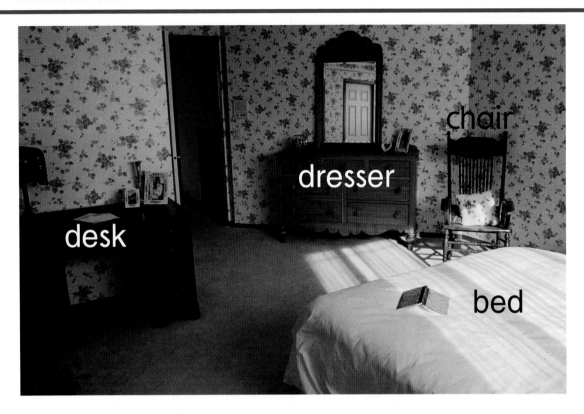

desk

dresser

chair

bed

Bathroom

bathtub

sink

toilet

Instruments

Musical

drum

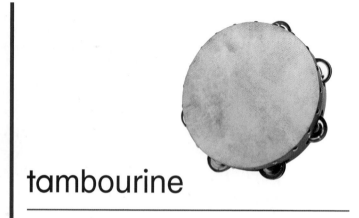

tambourine

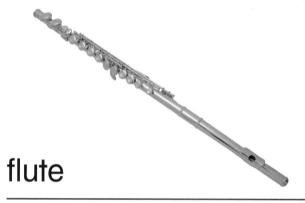

flute

trumpet

guitar

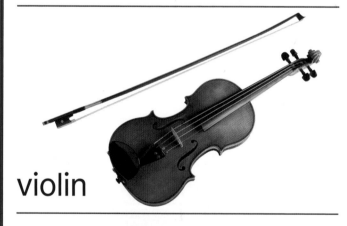

violin

piano

xylophone

Drawing and Writing

brush

markers

chalk

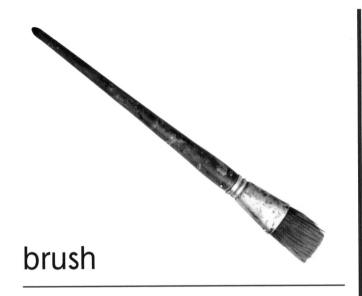

pen

crayons

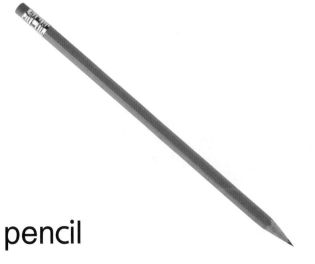

pencil

Tools

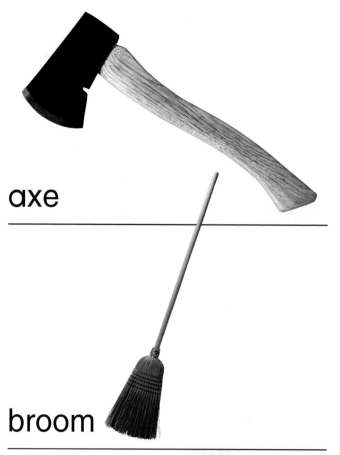

axe

broom

drill

flashlight

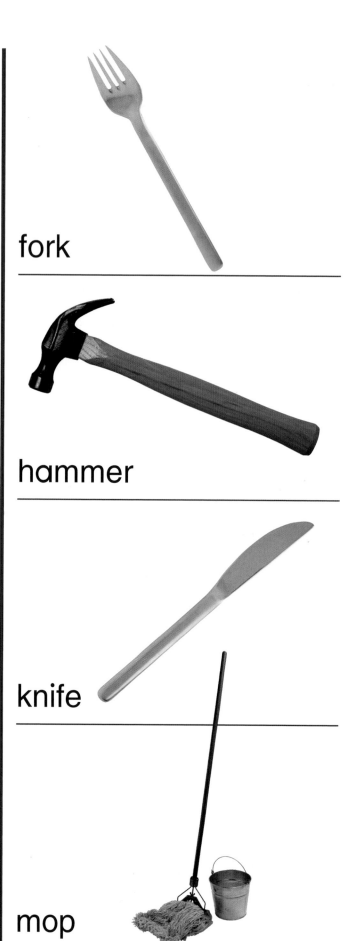

fork

hammer

knife

mop

paintbrush

screwdriver

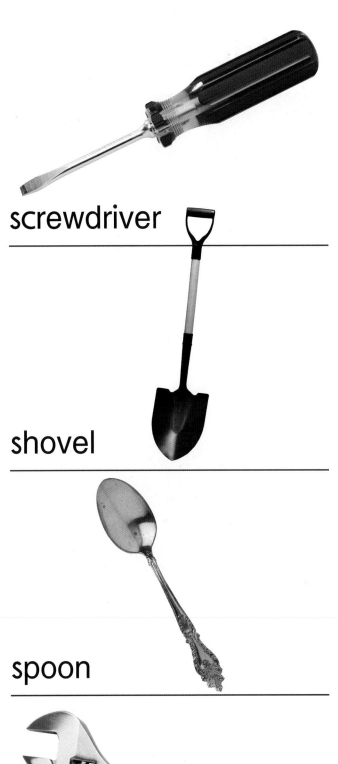

rake

shovel

saw

spoon

scissors

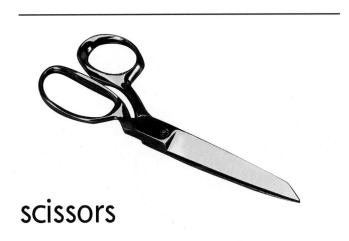

wrench

Machines

Outdoors

backhoe

lawn mower

bulldozer

snowblower

crane

tractor

Machines

Indoors

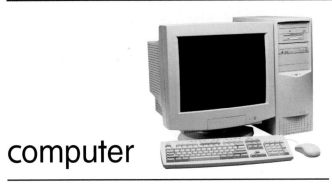

computer

hair dryer

microwave oven

radio

sewing machine

telephone

toaster

vacuum cleaner

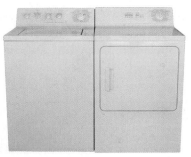

washer and dryer

Transportation

airplane

bus

bicycle

car

boat

elevated train

Transportation

helicopter

train

motorcycle

truck

subway

van

People and Their Jobs

astronaut

clerk

builder

construction worker

People and Their Jobs

cook

doctor

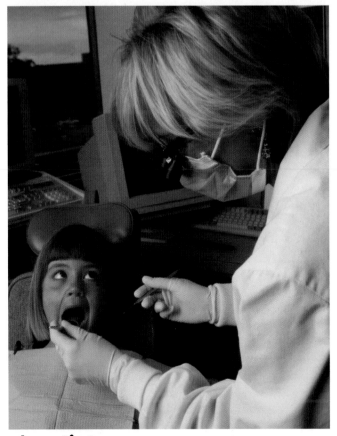

dentist

driver

People and Their Jobs

engineer

farmer

firefighter

hairdresser

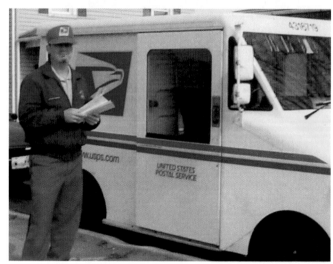

mail carrier

People and Their Jobs

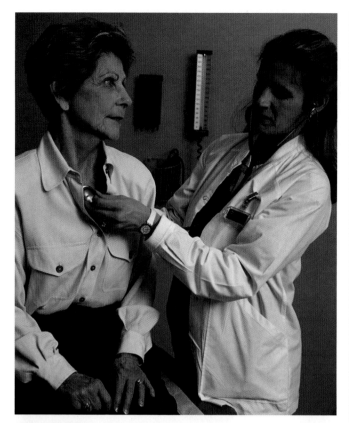

nurse

pilot

police officer

office worker

teacher

Buildings and Places

airport

city

apartment house

desert

bank

factory

farm and barns

hospital

garden

hotel

gym

library

Buildings and Places

museum

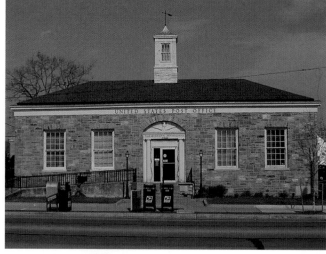

post office

park

ranch

playground

restaurant

Buildings and Places

school

store

skyscrapers

supermarket

stadium

theater

Opposites

big   little

front   back

clean   dirty

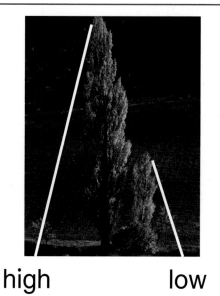

high   low

empty   full

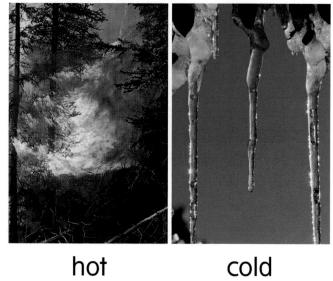

hot   cold

Opposites

short

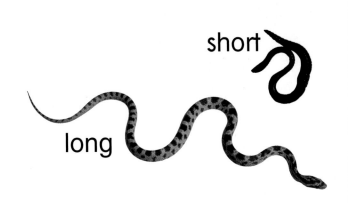

long

right   left

old

new

fast

slow

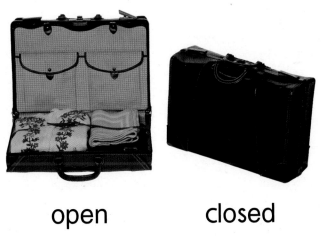

open   closed

wet

dry

Position Words

last   first

behind

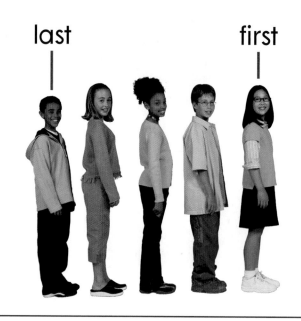

in front of

in   out

near   far

Position Words

on   off

over

under

up

down

Action Words

bend

clap

blow

climb

catch

count

Action Words

crawl

dig

cut

dive

dance

draw

Action Words

drink

fly

eat

hide

fall

hit

Action Words

hop

kiss

jump

knock

kick

lift

Action Words

listen

mix

look

paint

meet

play

Action Words

pull

ride

push

run

read

shout

Action Words

sing

slide

skate

smell

sleep

swim

Action Words

talk

wash

throw

win

walk

write

Picture Dictionary • Index